W9-DAE-604

A Walk With God

A Walk With God

Collected by
MICHAEL JAMES

STANYAN BOOKS

RANDOM HOUSE

Copyright ©, 1972, by
Montcalm Productions, Inc.

All rights reserved under
International Copyright Laws.

A Stanyan book
Published by Stanyan Books,
8721 Sunset Blvd., Suite C,
Hollywood, California 90069,
and by Random House, Inc.
201 East 50th Street,
New York, N.Y. 10022

Printed in U.S.A.

Designed by Hy Fujita

ISBN: 0-394-48058-9

Library of Congress Catalog
Card Number: 71-182684

For
IVY CRANE WILSON,
who never forgot

What we make in our minds
we call God, but in reality He
dwells in our hearts.

—WINSTON CHURCHILL

Let all those that put their trust in
Thee rejoice: let them ever shout for
joy, because Thou defendest them.

—PSALM 5:11

Behold, I send an Angel before
thee, to keep thee in the way, and
to bring thee into the place
which I have prepared.

—EXODUS 23:20

God walks with any man who
wants Him to.

—JIMI HENDRIX

He is with us always.
Remember that and be comforted.
— **KATHRYN KUHLMAN**

Great God, I ask Thee
for no meaner pelf
Than that I may not disappoint myself;
That in my action I may soar as high
as I can now discern
with this clear eye.
— **HENRY DAVID THOREAU**

How precious also are Thy
thoughts unto me, O God! how
great is the sum of them.
— **PSALMS 139:17**

Are You running with me, Jesus?
— **MALCOLM BOYD**

We must learn that to expect God
to do everything while we do nothing
is not faith, but superstition.
— **MARTIN LUTHER KING, JR.**

God, help me keep a resolution
that I make today: not to walk
head high even one more time
past someone I can help.

—ROD McKUEN

Live among men as if God
beheld you; speak with God as if
men were listening.
—**SENECA**

God? The imagination reels.
—**CHARLES AZNAVOUR**

Prayer shows us more clearly
than we saw before, what we already
have and are; and most of all,
it shows us what God is. Advancing
in this light, we reflect it; and this
light reveals the pure Mind-pictures,
in silent prayer, even as photography
grasps the solar light to portray
the face of pleasant thought.
—**MARY BAKER EDDY**

God is our refuge and strength,
a very present help in trouble.
— PSALMS 46:1

Lean on me, God,
I've leaned against You too long.
— DICK POWELL

Faith cometh by hearing,
and hearing by the word of God.
—ROMANS 10:17

Begin prayer by recalling
the presence of God. You will soon
feel the benefit of such a practice.
God is everywhere. There is no
place where He is not. Let birds
fly where they will, they always
encounter air; so we are always
where God is.

—ST. FRANCOIS DE SALES

I owe God so much
that paying Him back
will take a long time.

—JUDY GARLAND

Don't let go of me, God,
hold on a bit longer.

—CHARLES DeGAULLE

**God is everybody's friend...
or He should be.**
—HUMPHREY BOGART

Great is our responsibility
toward our fellow man;
greater is our responsibility
toward our Father.

— H. B. DEAN

At times when we are tempted
to complain, keep us mindful
of the light kindled by others,
and help us, our Father,
to keep the light burning
for the generations coming on.

— HAROLD BLAKE WALKER

Love, being the right hand of God,
should be dealt with courteously.

— ROD McKUEN

And the tree of the field
shall yield her fruit, and the earth
shall yield her increase, and they
shall be safe in their land, and shall
know that I am the Lord.

— EZEKIEL 34 : 27

Thy rod and thy staff they
comfort me.

— PSALMS 23:4

It is wrong to say that God made
rich and poor; He made only
male and female, and He gave them
the whole earth for their inheritance.

— THOMAS PAINE

The landing on the moon
will have no more to do with
theology, God, or self-knowledge
than any flower we pluck
or any hand we press — in fact,
much less.

— GEORGE SIMPSON

There is no scientific reason
why God cannot retain the same
position in our modern world
that He held before we began
probing His creation with telescope
and cyclotron.

—WERNHER von BRAUN

When the sun shines,
what man fears God
or His one begotten son.
— ROD McKUEN

Fear God,
and your enemies will fear you.
— BENJAMIN FRANKLIN

The love of God is infinite
for every human soul because
every human soul is unique.
No other can satisfy the same need
in God.
— WILLIAM BUTLER YEATS

We expect too much of God,
but He always seems ready.
— JOHN F. KENNEDY

WITH GOD ON OUR SIDE...

—BOB DYLAN

We cannot bridge the gap
between God and ourselves
through even the most intensive
and frequent prayers; the gap
between God and ourselves
can only be bridged by God.

— **PAUL TILLICH**

Blessed is he
who hungers for friends —
for though he may not realize it,
his soul is crying out for God.

— **HABIB SAHABIB**

Not believe in God?
You might just as well not believe
in anything. Some men don't,
you know, and I wonder how
these same men are able
to believe in themselves.

— MICHAEL JAMES

The thankful heart is the only door
that opens to God.

— JOE ORTON

I firmly believe in Divine Providence.
Without it, I think I should go crazy.
Without God the world would
be a maze without a clue.

— WOODROW WILSON

God gives grace to the humble.
— **MARY PICKFORD**

My God shall supply all your need
according to His riches in glory
by Christ Jesus.
— **PHILLIPPIANS 4:19**

God, if You're listening,
talk to me and walk with me.
(Last words of ANGELA DAYCO)

The love of God makes all men free.
— **BABE RUTH**

My presence shall go with thee,
and I will give thee rest.
— **EXODUS 33 : 14**

God is black and yellow and white
and young and old and smiling
and frowning. Just, but never unjust.
— SERGE MILINKOFF

We grumble because God put
thorns with roses; wouldn't it be
better to thank God that He put
roses with thorns?
— O. S. MARDEN

Oh God, our help in ages past,
our hope for years to come;
Be Thou our guard while troubles last,
and our eternal home.
— ISAAC WATTS

I discovered God
and only then myself.
— **PAT BOONE**

God's greatness lives in all free men.
— **HARRY S. TRUMAN**

If God had pleased to do so,
He would surely have made you
all one people. Instead, He tests you
by observing your use of the talents
He has given to each of you.
Emulate each other, then,
in good deeds, for to God you shall
all return.
—**THE KORAN**

I didn't see God...
but I saw the evidence that God lives.
—ASTRONAUT FRANK BORMAN

And this commandment have we
from Him, that he who loveth God
love his brother also.
— **1 JOHN 4:14-21**

The Lord is my rock, and my
fortress, and my deliverer.
— **2 SAMUEL 22:2**

Truth is God's daughter.
— **SPANISH PROVERB**

All things are passing,
God never changes.
— HENRY W. LONGFELLOW

Whither thou goest I will go;
and whither thou lodgest I will lodge;
thy people shall be my people
and thy God my God.
—RUTH 1:16

I like God, I hope He likes me.
—A THIRD GRADER

And God said, Let there be
light: and there was light.

— GENESIS 1:3

I say, All is in God; all
lives and moves in God.

— BENEDICT SPINOZA

Love thy neighbor.

— LEVITICUS 19:18

Let the words of my mouth, and
the meditation of my heart, be
acceptable in Thy sight.

— PSALMS 19:14

Seek the Lord, and ye shall live;
...Seek Him that maketh the seven
stars and Orion, and turneth the
shadow of death into the morning.

—AMOS 5:6, 8

I walk with God daily.

— HELEN KELLER

The ways of the Lord are right,
and the just shall walk in them.

—HOSEA 14:9

An evangelist is the man
who stands at the gates
of the Kingdom of Heaven and says,
"Come in."
—BILLY GRAHAM

I know as much about the afterlife
as you do—nothing.
I must wait and see.
—WILLIAM INGE

Something of God

I hear and behold God in every
object, yet understand God not
in the least,
Nor do I understand who there can
be more wonderful than myself.
Why should I wish to see God better
than this day?
I see something of God each hour
of the twenty-four, and each
moment then,
In the faces of men and women I see
God, and in my own face in the glass,
I find letters from God dropped
in the street, and every one is
signed by God's name,
And I leave them where they are, for
I know that wheresoe'er I go
Others will punctually come
forever and ever.
—WALT WHITMAN

Fields of wonder are the places
God goes walking in.
— ROD McKUEN

We are God's children
and He knows us and cares
about us — each of us.
—MRS. MARTIN LUTHER KING

I know that, whatsoever God doeth,
it shall be forever; nothing can be
put to it, nor anything taken from it.
—ECCLESIASTES 3:14

He who loves his fellow man
is loving God the best he can.
—ALICE CAREY

Nature is the art of God.
—SIR THOMAS BROWNE

Never lose an opportunity
to see anything beautiful.
Beauty is God's handwriting.
— CHARLES KINGSLEY

Rest assured you can never lack
God's outstretched arm so long
as you are in His service.
—MARY BAKER EDDY

The Supreme God is a Being
eternal, infinite, absolutely perfect.

— **ISAAC NEWTON**

We hold upon this earth the
place of Almighty God.

— **POPE LEO XIII**

Whoever falls from God's right
hand is caught in his left.

— **EDWIN MARKHAM**

The presence of a superior reasoning
power revealed in the
incomprehensible universe, forms
my idea of God.

—**ALBERT EINSTEIN**

A noble deed is a step toward God.
— J. G. HOLLAND

Ye shall not go out with haste,
nor go by flight; for the Lord will go
before you; and the God of Israel
will be your reward.
— ISAIAH 52:12

I believe in God—yet still I wonder.
Awe sometimes leads to disbelief.
— GEORGE BERNARD SHAW

The Lord bless thee, and keep thee:
The Lord make His face shine
upon thee, and be gracious
unto thee; The Lord lift up His
countenance upon thee, and give
thee peace.

—NUMBERS 6: 24, 25, 26

No one is so good but that he
has been touched by sin. No one is
so bad but that he can be reached
by the Saviour. "Your heavenly
Father will forgive you."

—H. B. DEAN

He can hear you all right,
but He ain't gonna listen unless you
talk straight to Him.

—ETHEL WATERS

We need a whole
lot more of Jesus
and a lot less
Rock and Roll...

— SONG

Thy will be done.

—LUKE 11:2